DEDICATED TO

ALL THE CHILDREN
AND GROWNUPS WHO
LOVE TO COLOR

Little Miss HISTORY COLORING BOOK, Volume I
© 2016 Barbara Ann Mojica. All Rights Reserved.
Published in The UNITED STATES of AMERICA
eugenus STUDIOS, LLC
P.O. BOX 112
CRARYVILLE, NY 12521
E-Mail: Barbara@LittleMissHistory.com
WebSite: www.LittleMissHISTORY.com

ISBN-13: 978-0-9885030-9-0
ISBN-10: 0988503093

BARBARA ANN MOJICA'S

Little Miss HISTORY®

VOLUME 1

COLORING BOOK

ILLUSTRATIONS BY VICTOR RAMON MOJICA

"BETTER TO REMAIN SILENT
AND BE THOUGHT A FOOL
THAN TO SPEAK OUT AND
REMOVE ALL DOUBT."

ABRAHAM LINCOLN

ABE AND MARY LINCOLN

"WHAT ARE ACTORS,
ANYWAY? MUMMERS OF THE
QUALITY OF SKIMMED MILK.
THEY KNOW LITTLE, THINK
LESS, AND UNDERSTAND
NEXT TO NOTHING."

JOHN WILKES BOOTH

JOHN WILKES BOOTH

"NEVER BE HAUGHTY TO THE HUMBLE OR HUMBLE TO THE HAUGHTY."

JEFFERSON DAVIS

JEFFERSON DAVIS

"GREATNESS BE NOTHING
UNLESS IT BE LASTING."

NAPOLEON BONAPARTE

BLASTING AT MOUNT RUSHMORE

"MY PURPOSE IS TO MAKE
MY NARRATIVE AS TRUTHFUL
AS POSSIBLE."

GEORGE ARMSTRONG CUSTER

U.S. CALVARY OFFICER

"I WAS BORN ON THE PRAIRIES WHERE THE WIND BLEW FREE AND THERE WAS NOTHING TO BREAK THE LIGHT OF THE SUN. I WAS BORN WHERE THERE WERE NO ENCLOSURES."

GERONIMO

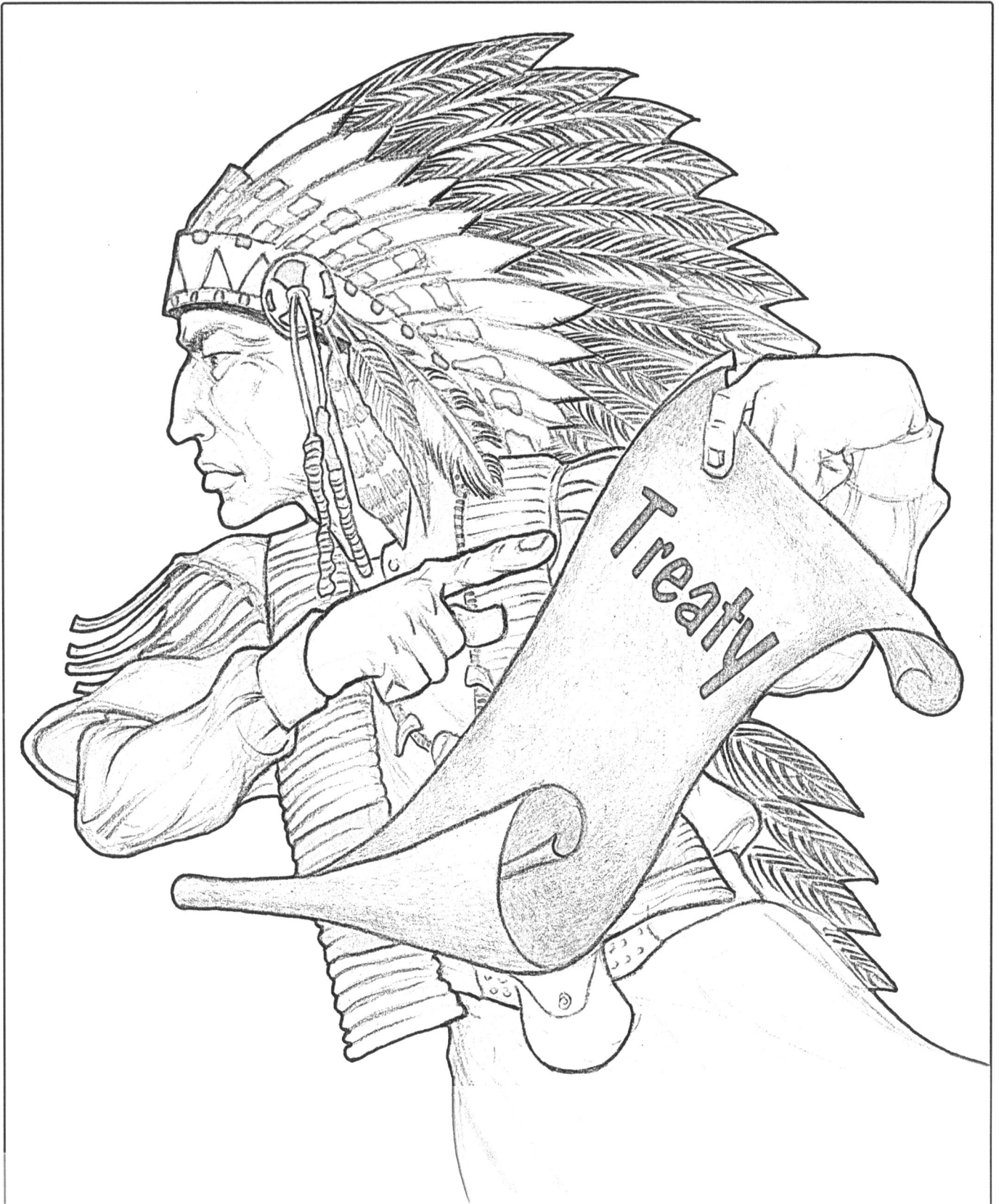

NATIVE AMERICAN CHIEF

"WHEN YOU REACH THE END
OF YOUR ROPE, TIE A KNOT
IN IT AND HANG ON."

FRANKLIN D. ROOSEVELT

FRANKLIN D. ROOSEVELT

"BE STEADY AND WELL-ORDERED IN YOUR LIFE SO THAT YOU CAN BE FIERCE AND ORIGINAL IN YOUR WORK."

GUSTAVE FLAUBERT

JACK FIXED WAGONS AT MOUNT VERNON

"HUMANITY HAS WON ITS BATTLE. LIBERTY NOW HAS A COUNTRY."

MARQUIS DE LAFAYETTE

MARQUIS DE LAFAYETTE

"I GREW UP IN AN IMMIGRANT
NEIGHBORHOOD. WE JUST
KNEW THE RULE WAS YOU'RE
GOING TO HAVE TO WORK
TWICE AS HARD."

LIN-MANUEL MIRANDA

ARRIVING AT ELLIS ISLAND

"AVIATION IS PROOF THAT
GIVEN THE WILL, WE HAVE
THE CAPACITY TO ACHIEVE
THE IMPOSSIBLE."

EDDIE RICKENBACKER

LITTLE MISS HISTORY
AS A WORLD WAR II PILOT

"WHERE YOU HAVE A PLOT OF LAND, HOWEVER SMALL, PLANT A GARDEN. STAYING CLOSE TO THE SOIL IS GOOD FOR THE SOUL."

SPENCER W. KIMBALL

IN GEORGE WASHINGTON'S GARDEN

"GIVE A GIRL THE RIGHT SHOES, AND SHE CAN CONQUER THE WORLD."

MARILYN MONROE

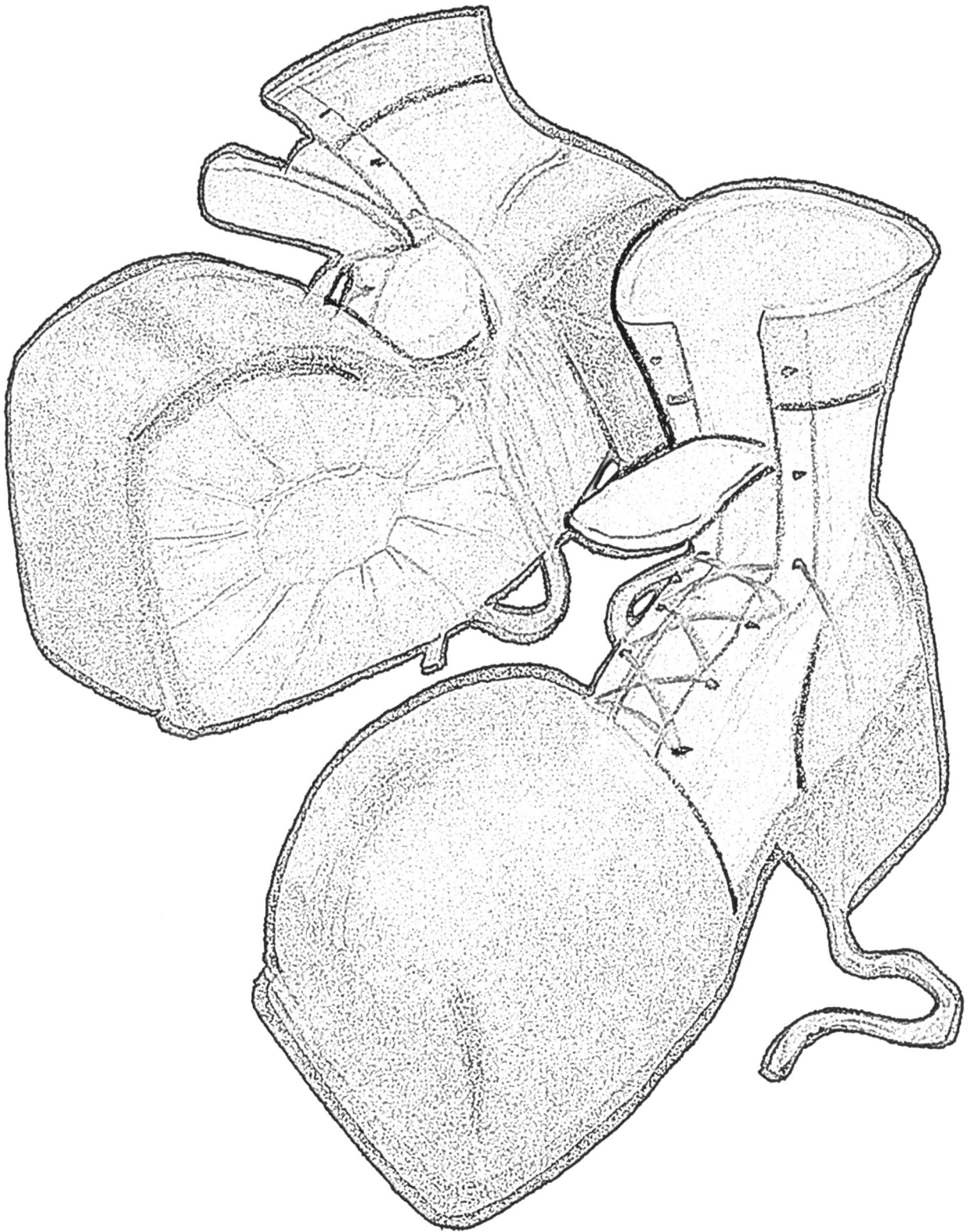

LITTLE MISS HISTORY'S BOOTS

"THE KITCHEN OVEN
IS RELIABLE, BUT IT'S
MADE US LAZY."

JAMIE OLIVER

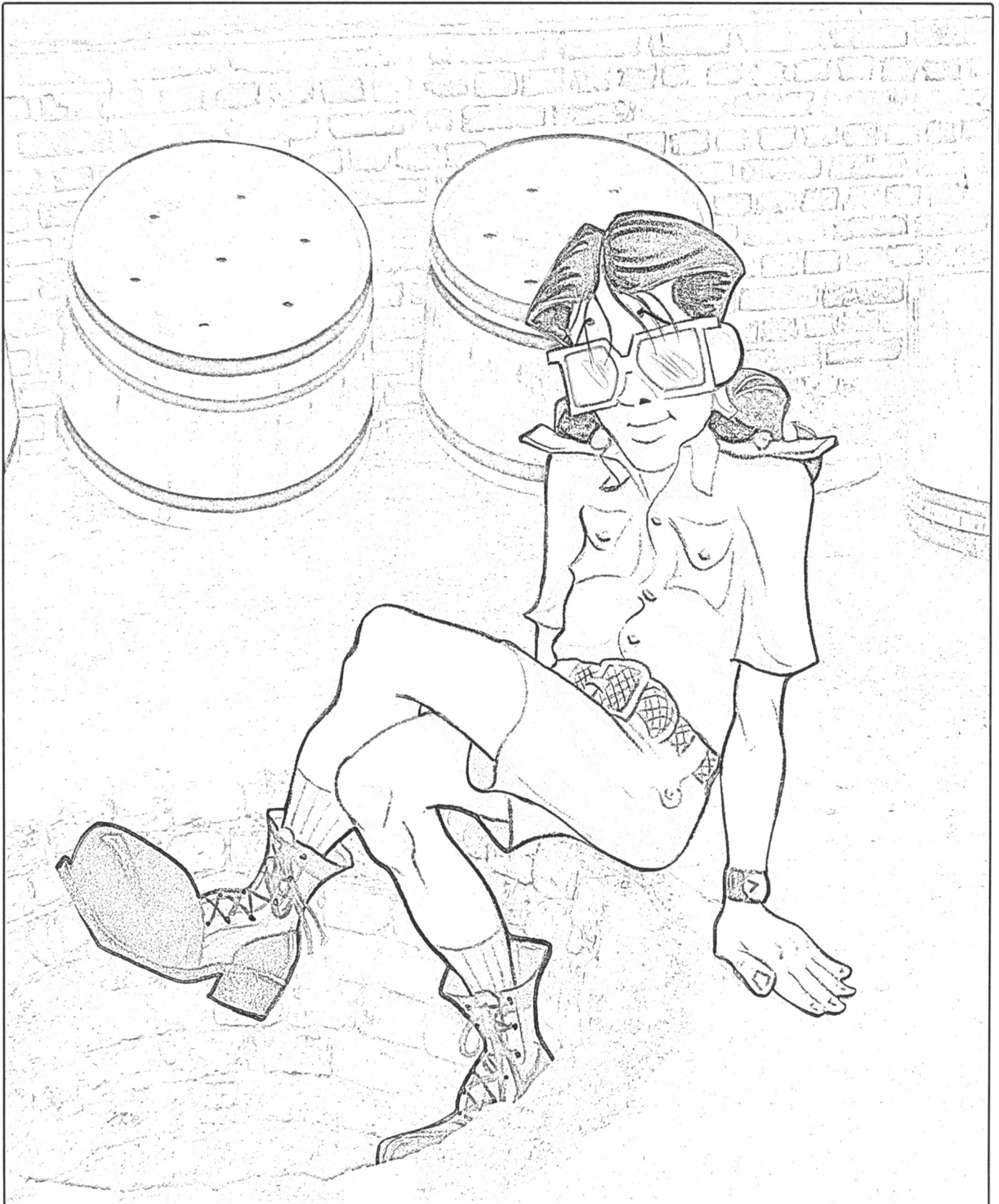

IN GEORGE WASHINGTON'S SMOKEHOUSE

"VISION IS THE ART
OF SEEING WHAT IS
INVISIBLE TO OTHERS."

JONATHAN SWIFT

SEEING THE WORLD THROUGH
ROSE COLORED GLASSES

"NO HOUR OF LIFE IS
WASTED THAT IS SPENT
IN THE SADDLE."

WINSTON CHURCHILL

LITTLE MISS HISTORY RIDING THROUGH
SEQUOIA NATIONAL PARK

"IF AT FIRST YOU DON'T SUCCEED, SKYDIVING IS NOT FOR YOU!"

HENNY YOUNGMAN

LITTLE MISS HISTORY SKYDIVING

"FROM BIRTH, MAN CARRIES
THE WEIGHT OF GRAVITY ON
HIS SHOULDERS. HE IS BOLTED
TO EARTH. BUT MAN HAS
ONLY TO SINK BENEATH THE
SURFACE AND HE IS FREE."

JACQUES COUSTEAU

LITTLE MISS HISTORY SCUBA DIVING

"SOMEONE IS SITTING IN THE SHADE TODAY BECAUSE SOMEONE PLANTED A TREE A LONG TIME AGO."

WARREN BUFFETT

GENERAL SHERMAN TREE

"WAR IS TOO SERIOUS
A MATTER TO
LEAVE TO SOLDIERS."

WILLIAM TECUMSEH SHERMAN

WILLIAM TECUMSEH SHERMAN

"KNOWING TREES, I
UNDERSTAND THE MEANING
OF PATIENCE. KNOWING
GRASS, I CAN APPRECIATE
PERSISTENCE."

HAL BORLAND

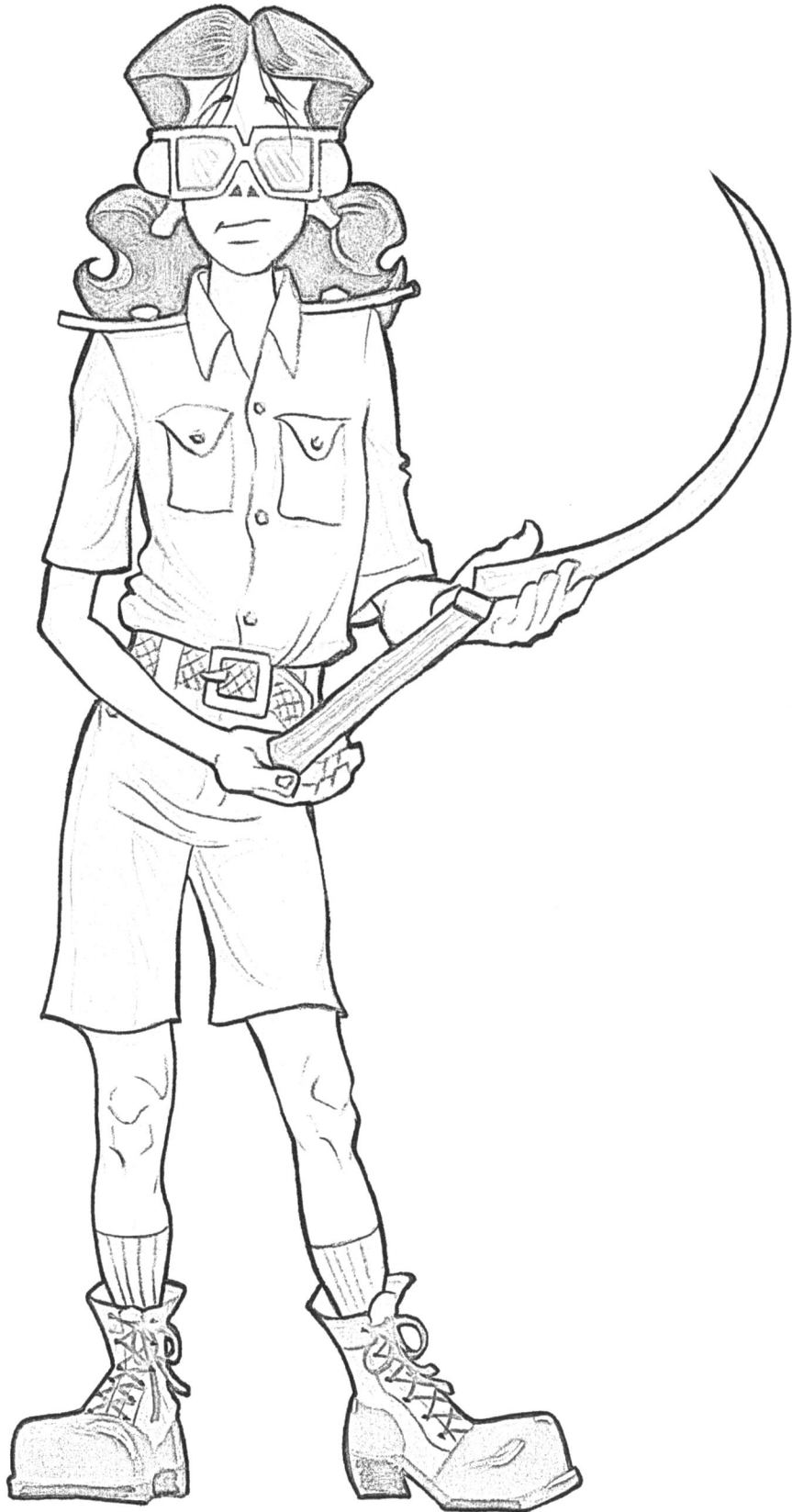

LITTLE MISS HISTORY HOLDING A
SCYTHE USED FOR CUTTING GRASS

"WHENEVER I HEAR ANYONE
ARGUING FOR SLAVERY, I FEEL
A STRONG IMPULSE TO SEE IT
TRIED ON HIM PERSONALLY."

ABRAHAM LINCOLN

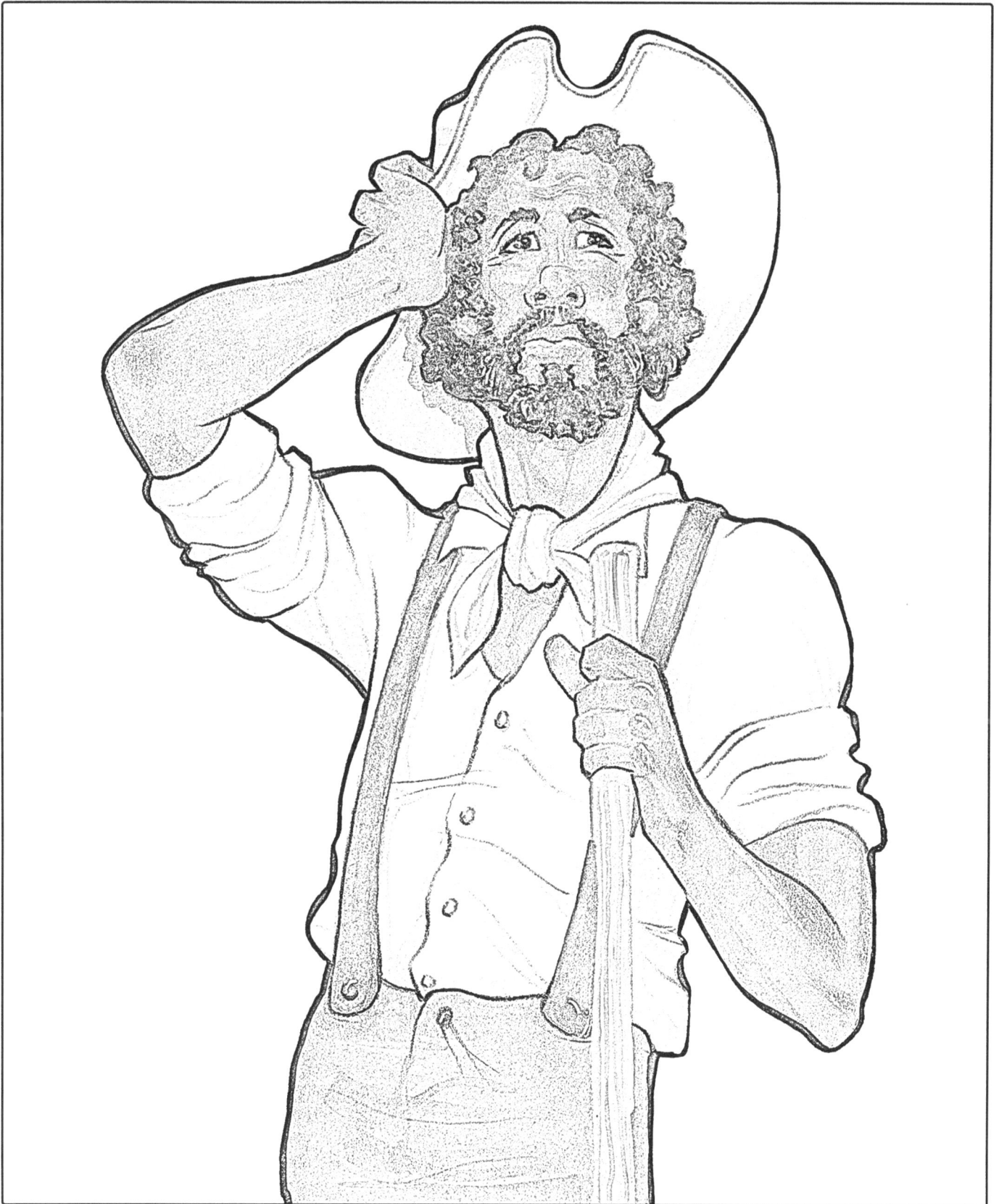

SLAVE WORKING AT MOUNT VERNON

"I CAN'T CHANGE THE
DIRECTION OF THE WIND,
BUT I CAN ADJUST MY SAILS
TO ALWAYS REACH MY
DESTINATION."

JIMMY DEAN

THE WIND SPREADING
SEQUOIA TREE SEEDS

"IT IS BETTER TO OFFER NO
EXCUSE THAN A BAD ONE."

GEORGE WASHINGTON

YOUNG OFFICER GEORGE WASHINGTON

"WHAT SCULPTURE IS TO A
BLOCK OF MARBLE, EDUCATION
IS TO THE SOUL."

JOSEPH ADDISON

STEPS ONCE USED BY WORKERS
TO REACH MOUNT RUSHMORE

"IT'S A RECESSION
WHEN YOUR NEIGHBOR
LOSES HIS JOB;
IT'S A DEPRESSION WHEN
YOU LOSE YOURS."

HARRY S. TRUMAN

HARRY S. TRUMAN

"DISOBEDIENCE IS THE TRUE
FOUNDATION OF LIBERTY. THE
OBEDIENT MUST BE SLAVES."

HENRY DAVID THOREAU

SLAVE WORKING AT MOUNT VERNON

"THE SOLUTION OFTEN
TURNS OUT MORE BEAUTIFUL
THAN THE PUZZLE."

RICHARD DAWKINS

Without re-arranging letters, how many words are there in the word "HISTORY"? I found 8.

1. _____

2. _____

3. _____

4. _____

5. _____

6. _____

7. _____

8. _____

Special thanks to
Stephen Wooten, and his
Coloring Book Creator
software, for helping to make
this book possible.

www.ingramcontent.com/pod-product-compliance
Lightning Source LLC
LaVergne TN
LVHW072119070426
835511LV00002B/21